THE BEST OF
MATT
2025

'Is it a "swarm" or a "flock" of trampolines?'

MATTHEW PRITCHETT
studied at St Martin's School of Art in London and first saw himself published in the *New Statesman* during one of its rare lapses from high seriousness. He has been the *Daily Telegraph*'s front-page pocket cartoonist since 1988. In 1995, 1996, 1999, 2005, 2009 and 2013 he was the winner of the Cartoon Arts Trust Award and in 1991, 2004 and 2006 he was 'What the Papers Say' Cartoonist of the Year. In 1996, 1998, 2000, 2008, 2009, 2018 and 2019 he was the *UK Press* Cartoonist of the Year and in 2015 he was awarded the Journalists' Charity Award. In 2002 he received an MBE.

Own your favourite Matt cartoons. Browse the full range of Matt cartoons and buy online at www.telegraph.co.uk/mattprints or call 0191 6030178.

The Telegraph
THE BEST OF
MATT
2025

'Any old AI can write a novel, but it takes a human to have writer's block'

SEVEN DIALS

An Orion Paperback

First published in Great Britain in 2025 by Seven Dials
A division of the Orion Publishing Group Ltd
Carmelite House
50 Victoria Embankment
London
EC4Y 0DZ

An Hachette UK Company

The authorised representative in the EEA is Hachette Ireland,
8 Castlecourt Centre, Dublin 15, D15 XTP3, Ireland (email: info@hbgi.ie)

10 9 8 7 6 5 4 3 2 1

© 2025 Telegraph Media Group Holdings Limited

The right of Matthew Pritchett to be identified as the author
of this work has been asserted in accordance with the
Copyright, Designs and Patents Act 1988.

All rights reserved. No part of this publication may be reproduced, stored
in a retrieval system or transmitted in any form or by any means, without
the prior permission in writing of the publisher, nor to be otherwise
circulated in any form of binding or cover other than that in which it is
published without a similar condition, including this condition, being
imposed on the subsequent purchaser.

A CIP catalogue record for this book is available from the British Library.

ISBN mmp: 978 1 3996 1045 2
ISBN ebook: 978 1 3996 1046 9

Printed in Italy by Elcograf, S.p.A

The Orion Publishing Group's policy is to use papers that are natural,
renewable and recyclable products and made from wood grown in
sustainable forests. The logging and manufacturing processes are expected
to conform to the environmental regulations of the country of origin.

www.orionbooks.co.uk

THE BEST OF MATT
2025

'Who owns us? Are we being given away? This must be what it feels like to work at the Daily Telegraph'

Prisons

'Your crime is important to us, but unfortunately you've been arrested at a particularly busy time ...'

Prisons

'The previous inmate marked the passing of time. As you can see, he was here for nearly an hour'

'Don't make me do another speed awareness course. Can I choose chemical castration instead?'

Alternatives to custodial sentences considered.

Prisons

'Will you return this overdue library book for me? As a white male I'd be facing a lengthy prison sentence'

'Prisons used to be universities of crime, but these days nobody's inside long enough to learn anything'

Prisons

Prisons

'I've booked you a cell on May 16th at 1pm, but we need it back by 3pm'

'I've baked a cake for the climate protesters in jail. I've hidden a tube of super glue inside'

Farming

'One day, son, all this will belong to HMRC'

'It's my new working dog. He's an inheritance tax expert'

Farming

'Farmers don't understand Treasury ways. Taxing them isn't cruel, they're stunned first and it's all over quickly'

Farming

'When they're lying down it means they've superglued themselves to the ground as part of a farming protest'

'While I was in London protesting, the Government built these houses on my land'

Farming

'A Frappuccino with oat milk and spiced caramel topping? London has changed you'

'I like my eggs free-range, but I don't think farmers should be allowed to roam free around London'

Labour

'Surprisingly, Robin, nobody likes your plan to steal from pensioners to give to train drivers'

'Don't blow out the candles. They warm up the room and we've lost our winter fuel payment'

Labour

'Do you still wear this suit? I'm sending a bag of clothes to 10 Downing Street'

'The PM wants to watch a film. Can he use your Netflix account?'

Freebies row. Ministers receive free clothes and concert tickets.

Labour

'There are three groups on the Labour benches. The hard left, the Blairites and the Swifties'

'A police escort for the Prime Minister? Have you cleared this with Taylor Swift's mother?'

Freebies row. Ministers receive free clothes and concert tickets.

'I'm surprised Taylor Swift isn't here. Keir Starmer goes to all her shows'

'Next is a heart-wrenching song about a Prime Minister who is forced to pay for his own Taylor Swift tickets'

Freebies row. Ministers receive free clothes and concert tickets.

Labour

Labour

'Specialist subject: all the corrections that Rachel Reeves has made to her CV'

'If inflation keeps rising Rachel Reeves will remove "Chancellor of the Exchequer" from her CV'

Labour

'My accountant told me to dig up all the nuts and eat them before the budget'

'Now I've seen the budget details, I no longer think uncertainty is the worst thing for businesses'

Labour

'I miss the days when Labour politicians would just punch the public in the face'

Death of John Prescott.

'Before US tariffs we carried 220,000 tons of goods. Today we're taking a jar of Marmite and a packet of shortbread biscuits to America'

Labour

'The worst thing about our government's blunders is that we can't properly enjoy all France's problems'

'Like Facebook and X we've decided to get rid of fact checkers'

Labour

'We're going to reduce illegal immigration by imposing a four day working week on the people-smuggling gangs'

'We're so determined to cut costs we've set up two departments to tackle Government waste'

Labour

Labour

'Angela Rayner tried to resolve the bins dispute and now the rats have gone on strike'

Birmingham bin strike.

Birmingham bin strike.

Labour

'I didn't actually study law, I just identify as a Supreme Court judge'

'The white smoke means that Keir Starmer has decided what a woman is'

Labour

'I can't keep up. A few weeks ago a female pensioner could have a penis, but not a winter fuel payment ...'

'This used to be an all-male society, but then Keir Starmer said a woman CAN have a magic wand'

Labour

'Your flight leaves from our new runway. Start walking to Gate 196 and it should be built by the time you get there'

'Sadiq Khan has made it a Low-Traffic Runway'

Labour

'This is the environmental impact report on the third runway. Give it to our baggage handlers and ask them to lose it'

'We now think it was where people came to argue about a third runway at Heathrow'

Labour

'Harvest Festival is different nowadays in the green belt'

'Angela Rayner obtained a compulsory purchase order for the pitch'

'If it gets any colder Angela Rayner will build 1.5m igloos all over the UK'

Labour

Labour

'There's an eerie cold spot here. I feel the presence of a heat pump'

'Net zero rules mean I've had to replace the gunpowder with a heat pump'

Heat pump controversy.

Labour

'One day, son, all 10 recycling bins will be yours'

'It's a school project. I have to pull up this mustard and cress and install a solar farm'

Labour

'We took back control, but they took back all the mackerel, sole and haddock'

'Let's not get him a pet passport. His Instagram posts are already insufferable'

Building bridges with Europe.

Labour

'This deal means the UK can export to India some of our most successful products – like chicken tikka masala'

'I've been panic buying steel'

Government steps in to save steel industry.

Working from Home

Working from Home

'When I'm working from home I mostly do fire drills'

'We employ only British workers. The residents look after themselves while our staff work from home'

Motoring

Jaguar cars advert features no cars.

Trump Wins

'I used to enjoy observing Earth, but recently the storylines have become too far-fetched'

'He'd set his heart on storming the Capitol'

Trump Wins

Trump's Tariffs

'That "Make America Great Again" hat is now $100. It's made in China'

'If US stock markets keep falling we might be able to buy America soon'

'I think it was Confucius who said "A man who imposes tariffs of 104 per cent is dumber than a sack of bricks"'

'Good evening, and welcome to "What's Trump Done Now?"'

Trump's Tariffs

Ukraine

'Let this be a warning to China. If they invade Taiwan they'll only be allowed to keep some of it'

'Could we offer Ukraine off-peak membership of Nato? We'll defend them, but not at very busy times'

Ukraine

'Make sure the meeting is on the ground floor. You never know when someone might fall out of a window'

Ukraine

Ukraine

'The chancellor has approved your latest spending request. Would you like milk in it?'

'Publish the date of the jumble sale, but not the US bombing plans. Those were sent to us by mistake'

Military secrets leaked.

Tory Troubles

'A war has broken out in the Tory Party between the "unity" fanatics and the "work together" nutters'

'Ask yourself: is this the leader I want to be writing a letter of no confidence about after six months?'

Tory Troubles

'Don't vote for the candidate you promised to support; you'll mess up the whole system'

'They've re-booked this hall for 2029. I asked if they'd need more seats and they said probably not'

And Finally . . .

'You've been late every day this week. If it happens again you'll get a pay rise'

'I'm in favour of assisted dying if it means HS2 will be put out of its misery'

And Finally...

'Don't drive anywhere near the Treasury. You'll spook the money markets'

'I'm off work with anxiety. I'm terrified Rachel Reeves will come to my factory and I'll have to listen to her giving a speech'

Rachel Reeves' tears.

And Finally . . .

'He was building a straw house when he was crushed by a solar panel'

'If we call these new starter homes, the Government has almost hit its target'

And Finally...

'I got you a strawberry and cream sandwich and a gin and tonic baguette'

'Intense heat and a hot breeze. This isn't a bedroom, this is an air fryer'

And Finally . . .

'This invitation to the Jeff Bezos wedding was left behind our wheelie bins'

'The UK has agreed that its defence budget will be 5% of what Jeff Bezos is spending on his wedding'

And Finally . . .

'We had no idea wars were so expensive. How much for a skirmish?'

'The UK is getting 12 new submarines, but if the Russians come in small rubber boats it will be impossible to stop them'

And Finally . . .

Pro-Palestine protests.

And Finally . . .

'I tried to download the NHS App, but I accidentally paid for car parking in the High Street'

'Your appendix is like NHS England. You can survive perfectly well without it'

And Finally . . .

'When AI takes my job it will be shocked to see how much tax it has to pay'

'You've been replaced by new technology. They've developed a computer that doesn't work'

And Finally …

And Finally . . .

'We've added a talent contest to the papal conclave'

'It's better for the environment than our old stove, but nobody will know when we choose the next Pope'

And Finally…

'Reform is taking voters from Labour and the Conservatives. If Farage starts falling off paddleboards we're in trouble'

'With all the Reform Party infighting, we're trying to prevent a war between Clacton and Great Yarmouth'

And Finally . . .

'Do you want fries with that?'

'You're fabulously thin! You look like a jobless person who's been forced to have weight-loss jabs'

And Finally...

'We can turn things round. We've made mistakes, but that's all sewage under the bridge'

And Finally....

'Any minute now, Keir Starmer will leave £9bn somewhere round here'

'The book is free and you'll receive £101 million for the next 99 years'

And Finally …

And Finally . . .

'Elon Musk might find himself occupying Mars sooner than he expected'

Bromance over.

'The cause of the power cut was traced to a hotel room where a British family were charging their mobile phones, iPads, Kindles, laptops, cameras ...'

Spain suffers huge power cut.

And Finally . . .

Paris Olympics rocked by fires and animal cruelty accusations.

And Finally . . .

And Finally . . .

'The Post Office is closing this branch, so in future I'll have to send myself to prison'

Roses are red
And that's no lie
**** your bins
I hope you die
Anon MP

Minister resigns after abusive WhatsApp messages.

And Finally . . .

'The 8.17 made a number of pledges that it would now like to water down'

'It's not high speed any more. In fact, the replacement bus service cuts an hour off the journey time'

And Finally . . .

And Finally . . .

'Bad news about the £. Now it's caught the winter vomiting and diarrhoea bug'

And Finally . . .

'Has somebody upset Ed Miliband?'

'How much is a book of 12 first-class stamps? ... Would it be cheaper to buy the Royal Mail?'

And Finally . . .

Smoking ban in pub gardens considered.

And Finally …

Lauren Sánchez heads all-female crew in Jeff Bezos' rocket.

Lineker departs after social media post.

And Finally . . .

And Finally . . .

'Keir Starmer has a VOICE COACH? That's like Nigel Farage having a gym membership'

'Well, the assisted dying debate has become more acrimonious'

And Finally...

Dry January.